DINOSAUR WORLD

Bony Back

The Adventure of Stegosaurus

Written by Michael Dahl

Illustrated by Jeff Yesh

Thanks to our advisers for their expertise, research, knowledge, and advice:

Brent H. Breithaupt, Director
Geological Museum, University of Wyoming
Laramie, Wyoming

Peter Dodson, Ph.D.
Professor of Earth and Environmental Sciences
University of Pennsylvania
Philadelphia, Pennsylvania

Susan Kesselring, M.A.
Literacy Educator
Rosemount-Apple Valley-Eagan (Minnesota) School District

PICTURE WINDOW BOOKS
Minneapolis, Minnesota

Managing Editor: Bob Temple
Creative Director: Terri Foley
Editors: Nadia Higgins, Brenda Haugen
Editorial Adviser: Andrea Cascardi
Copy Editor: Laurie Kahn
Designer: Nathan Gassman
Page production: Picture Window Books
The illustrations in this book were rendered digitally.

Picture Window Books
5115 Excelsior Boulevard
Suite 232
Minneapolis, MN 55416
1-877-845-8392
www.picturewindowbooks.com

Printed in the United States of America.

Library of Congress Cataloging-in-Publication Data
Dahl, Michael.
Bony back : the adventure of stegosaurus / written by Michael Dahl ;
illustrated by Jeff Yesh.
p. cm. — (Dinosaur world)
Summary: Explains how scientists learn about dinosaurs and what their
discoveries have revealed about Stegosaurus.
Includes bibliographical references and index.
ISBN 1-4048-0135-9
1. Stegosaurus Juvenile literature. [1. Stegosaurus. 2. Dinosaurs.]
I. Yesh, Jeff, 1971- ill. II. Title.
QE862.O65 D62 2004
567.915'3—dc21
                                        2003004131

No humans lived during the time of the dinosaurs. No people heard them roar, saw their scales, or felt their feathers.

The giant creatures are gone, but their fossils, or remains, lie hidden in the earth. Dinosaur skulls, skeletons, and eggs have been buried in rock for millions of years.

All around the world, scientists dig up fossils and carefully study them. Bones show how tall the dinosaurs stood. Claws and teeth show how they grabbed and what they ate. Scientists compare fossils with the bodies of living creatures such as birds and reptiles, who are relatives of the dinosaurs. Every year, scientists learn more and more about the giants that have disappeared.

Studying fossils and figuring out how the dinosaurs lived is like putting together the pieces of a puzzle that is millions of years old.

This is what some of those pieces can tell us about the dinosaur known as Stegosaurus.

Night was coming to an end in the forest. Stars faded from the sky. A cool breeze sighed through the giant ferns.

4

Before the sun came up, a female Stegosaurus (stehg-uh-SAWR-us) already was feeding. Her tough bird-like beak ripped hundreds of leafy ferns from the ground.

Some scientists think Stegosaurus had cheek pouches, like a squirrel does. The pouches held plants that were waiting to be chewed.

Stegosaurus was a plant-eating dinosaur that grew to the size of a small pickup truck. Four scaly legs with tough, clawed toes held up a chunky body and a long, spiked tail.

The most impressive feature of Stegosaurus was a row of giant plates that grew along her back. Stegosaurus's nickname is Bony Back.

By noon, the sun was blazing down on the forest. In a small clearing, Stegosaurus nosed in the sand. She sniffed the spot where she had buried her eggs several weeks earlier. The sand had kept the eggs warm and safe.

Soon the eggs began to break open.

Some scientists believe that a mother Stegosaurus left her babies to hatch and grow up by themselves. Other scientists think Stegosaurus tended her young until they were able to feed themselves.

The baby Stegosauruses crawled out of the sand. They blinked in the bright sunlight. A row of bony bumps glistened on their backs.

The bumps soon would grow into giant bony plates like the ones on their mother's back. The largest plates, on the top of the spine, would become the size of car windows.

Stegosaurus means "roofed lizard" because of the roof of 17 plates the dinosaur carried on her back.

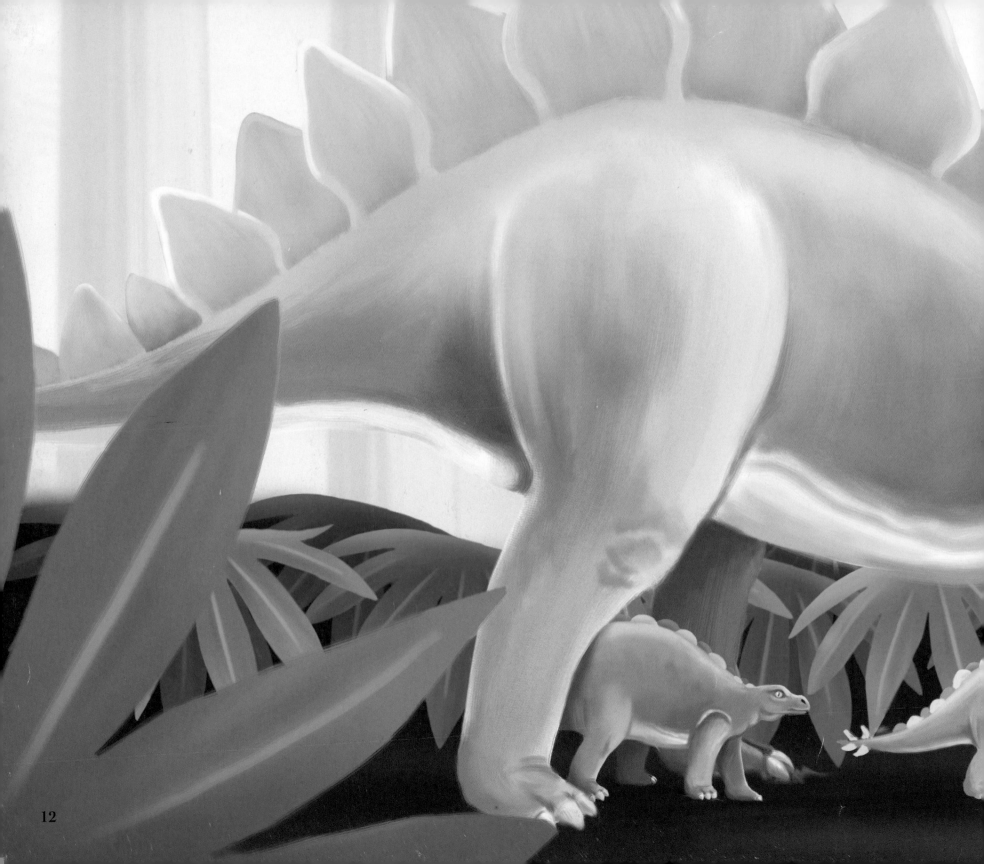

Stegosaurus bent over her hatchlings. Her small head felt hot in the sunlight. She shifted her back, catching a slight breeze. The cool air brushed against the thin skin of the plates. The breeze against Stegosaurus's plates helped her cool off.

The row of plates could warm up the dinosaur, too. Stegosaurus would turn her side toward the sun. As sunlight shone on the wide sides of the plates, it warmed the dinosaur's blood.

As the afternoon sun sank in the sky, Stegosaurus
heard a rustling noise in a thick row of ferns.
A quick sniff told her danger threatened
her babies. Her plates grew bright red.

Stegosaurus's plates were solid bone, filled with a web of blood vessels. A layer of thin skin covered each plate. When Stegosaurus grew angry or frightened, the plates changed color. The red color was a warning to enemies.

Some scientists believe Stegosaurus's plates may not have turned bright red. Like a chameleon's skin, the plates may have changed other colors—blue, green, yellow, or orange.

A pack of small two-legged meat-eaters slid out from the ferns. The creatures, called Ornitholestes (awr-nih-thuh-LEH-steez), fed on baby dinosaurs. Their gleaming eyes stared at the Stegosaurus hatchlings.

The mother Stegosaurus lashed her spiked tail back and forth. Several meat-eaters were knocked over the ferns. They fell, rolling in the dirt.

Stegosaurus lived with dangerous neighbors. Torvosaurus (tor-voh-SAWR-us), Ceratosaurus (seh-ra-tuh-SAWR-us), and Allosaurus (al-uh-SAWR-us) were among her many enemies.

17

18

Two of the meat-eaters opened their toothy jaws and ran at Stegosaurus. Their long arms clawed at Stegosaurus's neck.

But Stegosaurus was not harmed. Bony knobs in her neck protected her from enemy claws and teeth.

Some kinds of stegosaurs had sharp spikes growing from their shoulders.

A swift Ornitholestes gripped two hatchlings in his claws and scurried away. The remaining meat-eaters darted off to join their companion.

With the dangerous creatures gone, Stegosaurus lumbered toward a stand of ferns to feed, using her beak to pull at the greens. Stegosaurus munched quietly, but kept her babies close by her feet.

Stegosaurus: Where ...

In the United States, Stegosaurus remains have been found in Colorado, Oklahoma, Utah, and Wyoming.

... and When

The "Age of Dinosaurs" began 248 million years ago (mya). If we imagine the time from the beginning of the dinosaur age to the present as one day, dinosaurs lived almost 18 hours — and humans appeared just 10 minutes ago!

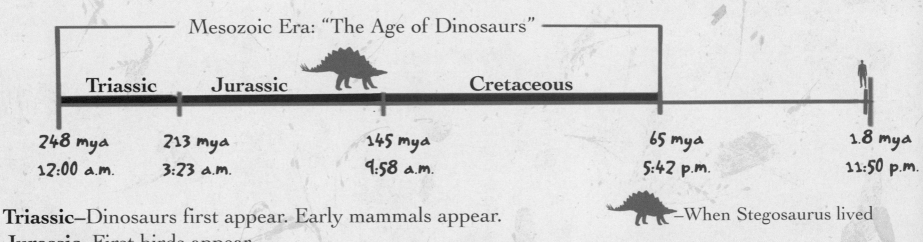

Mesozoic Era: "The Age of Dinosaurs"

Triassic	Jurassic		Cretaceous		
248 mya	213 mya	145 mya		65 mya	1.8 mya
12:00 a.m.	3:23 a.m.	9:58 a.m.		5:42 p.m.	11:50 p.m.

Triassic–Dinosaurs first appear. Early mammals appear.
Jurassic–First birds appear.
Cretaceous–Flowering plants appear. By the end of this era, all dinosaurs disappear.

–When Stegosaurus lived

–First humans appear

Digging Deeper

Plate Rows

Some scientists think Stegosaurus plates pointed straight up in one long line down its back. Other scientists think the plates stuck out a little to each side, growing in two separate rows. Different kinds of stegosaurs may have grown different numbers of back plates.

Eat and Run

A single full-grown Stegosaurus ate almost 300 pounds (140 kilograms) of plants every day. Most of the plants that grew in the days of the dinosaurs took a full year to grow back, so Stegosaurus always was moving and searching for new food.

Herd or Not

Some scientists think Stegosaurus was a herd animal that grazed in huge groups. The babies and young dinosaurs may have been kept in the middle of the herd, safe from prowling predators.

Funny Name

The group of spikes on the end of a Stegosaurus tail has been named the thagomizer. Scientists took the name from a cartoon by Gary Larson. In Larson's cartoon, cavemen talked about poor Thag Simmons, who was killed by the spikes on a Stegosaurus tail.

Words to Know

dinosaur—a land reptile that lived in prehistoric times. All dinosaurs died out millions of years ago.
fern—a leafy, flowerless plant
fossil—the remains of a plant or animal that lived between thousands and millions of years ago
hatchling—a baby animal that came out of an egg
spine—the backbone of an animal

To Learn More

At the Library

Cohen, Daniel. *Stegosaurus*. Mankato, Minn.: Bridgestone Books, 2001.

Fritz, Sandy, and George Olshevsky. *Stegosaurus*. North Mankato, Minn.: Smart Apple Media, 2003.

Holmes, Thom and Laurie. *Armored, Plated, and Bone-Headed Dinosaurs: The Ankylosaurs, Stegosaurs, and Pachycephalosaurs*. Berkeley Heights, N.J.: Enslow, 2002.

Landau, Elaine. *Stegosaurus*. New York: Children's Press, 1999.

On the Web

Enchanted Learning: Zoom Dinosaurs

http://www.EnchantedLearning.com/subjects/dinosaurs

For information, games, and jokes about dinosaurs, fossils, and prehistoric life

The Natural History Museum, London: Dino Directory

http://flood.nhm.ac.uk/cgi-bin/dino

For an alphabetical database of information on the Age of Dinosaurs

University of California, Berkeley: Museum of Paleontology

http://www.ucmp.berkeley.edu/museum/k-12.html

Online exhibits, articles, activities, and resources for teachers and students

Fact Hound

Fact Hound offers a safe, fun way to find Web sites related to this book. All of the sites on Fact Hound have been researched by our staff.

http://www.facthound.com

1. Visit the Fact Hound home page.
2. Enter a search word related to this book, or type in this special code: 1404801359.
3. Click on the FETCH IT button.

Your trusty Fact Hound will fetch the best sites for you!